John Graves
10/1/82

TEXAS HEARTLAND

Bluebonnets, prickly pears, and cedars (Ashe junipers)

TEXAS
HEARTLAND
A Hill Country Year

Photographs by JIM BONES, JR.

Text by JOHN GRAVES

TEXAS A&M UNIVERSITY PRESS  *College Station*

Composition by G & S Typesetters, Austin
Printing by Hart Graphics, Inc., Austin
Binding by Universal Bookbindery, Inc., San Antonio
Design by William D. Wittliff

Library of Congress Cataloging in Publication Data

Bones, Jim.
   Texas heartland.

1. Photography, Artistic. 2. Nature photography. 3. Texas—History.
I. Graves, John, 1920-   II. Title.
TR654.B663   779'.9'97640924   75-16352
ISBN 0-89096-002-X

Dedicated to

BERTHA McKEE DOBIE

J. FRANK DOBIE

EDGAR B. KINCAID, JR.

and to all they love

CONTENTS

THE REGION AND THE PLACE

John Graves When I was in college in the relatively innocent and provincial early 1940's, a group of us used to go for a long weekend every spring, with dates and faculty chaperones, to a place on the Balcones Escarpment where a little river gushed out full-size from big springs and ran clear and strong for a few miles before merging with the Guadalupe. It had steep cedar hills and fields gaudy with bluebonnets and fish and boats and streamside cypress trees and beerhalls run by pleasant Germans, and everything else you could have wanted it to have, and one day while a few of us were lying on grass in the spring sun by the river, a friend of mine from Houston said something which, while not especially profound, has recurred to me often since.

"This is where everybody would like to come from," he said. "There isn't a soul in Texas that wouldn't have been born here in these hills if he could have managed it."

As I recall, he got some argument on the subject out of a couple of localistic types from the Panhandle High Plains and the East Texas piney woods, but most of us just listened, because allowing for a little exaggeration he was somehow right. The Hill Country, that imprecisely defined crescent of deep-carved, layered limestone covering all or parts of several counties west and north of the Escarpment as it curves from Austin down through San Antonio and beyond, is revered as a sort of heartland by large numbers of Texans, even if they did not grow up there or anywhere nearby.

The region does lie quite close to the exact center of the state as established by those who establish such matters. But except for the geography of the thing, why this affectionate attitude should exist is at first glance puzzling. Few people, as people go nowadays, inhabit the Hill Country, which is not a very hospitable section from which to try to wrest a living. Agriculturally, with its mainly rocky terrain and its rather skimpy yield of cattle and sheep and goats and not much else, it is small potatoes in comparison with the state's rich blacklands just to the east, or the lush rainy prairies of the upper coast, or the irrigated High Plains, or the Rio Grande 11

Valley. It sits astraddle the thirty-inch line of average annual rainfall, which means that in good years there is enough moisture for adequate grazing on the hills and even for standard Eastern crops in the restricted patches of arable land, but means too that in other years—all too many of them—drouth shoulders in eastward from the big semi-arid Edwards Plateau on whose rim the Hill Country lies, and men and animals have to tough it out as best they can, and crops die.

Hardly any of it has railroad service—when the lines were being built, smoother alternative routes existed to east and west and north and south —and none of its highways can be called major. Its towns are small and not closely spaced, and in terms of business, for the most part, the entertainment of vacationers and deer-hunters and other pleasure-seekers tends to outweigh more serious commerce. Besides the ubiquitous limestone, a number of interesting and useful minerals crop out among the igneous and metamorphic formations of the queer intrusive Llano Uplift area, but the prosperity they engender is not startling. Nor has the sludge-like cash scent of petroleum, most Texan of minerals, ever hung heavy on the region's air.

Though it has ranches in plenty, the bulk of them are smallish places whose leathery operators do most of their own hard work, and within recent history have been more interested in sheep and Angora goats than in larger and more glamorous beasts. The range-cattle tradition does exist here, as in all of western Texas, but until the recent nationwide boom in cowboyism engendered by such stimuli as TV and rodeos and the conversion of humid croplands to beef pasture (and, I suppose, country music and hippie fashions and Marlboro cigarette ads and all that), the social tone of cafés and honky-tonks and courthouse squares in Blanco and Gillespie and Kerr and the other hill counties was more likely to be established by cedar-post choppers and raunchy goat-ranchers than by dandies in high heels and large belt-buckles. And a good many of these stylesetters—a majority in many places—were not out of the old Anglo-Texan stock but German in descent and proud of it, doing country things in ways that often traced back to Hesse or Alsace or Prussia, little concerned with specifically Texan manners and mores.

The Hill Country neither is nor was, in other words, a very typical chunk of Texas as the world at large and perhaps most Texans think of the state. Yet the fact that it nevertheless has a heartland aura and reputation is not really hard to explain. The Hill Country has charm and varied beauty of a sort that somehow tugs at the feelings of people from other, *John* different kinds of country. To East Texans out of damp windless forests, *Graves* it gives sculptured stone cliffs and ample views from high places and the clean feel of dry plateau air on their skins, and in the old days it gave them also a summer respite from malarial mosquitoes and such things. To people from the monotonous if rich prairie farming regions, it offers a new landscape at every turn in the road, and trees—live oak and cedar and Spanish oak and flowering shrubs on the hills, tall cypresses and hard-woods of a dozen species in the valleys. West Texans from the big, dry cattle country like these things too, and their long familiarity with creeks and riverbeds that have no water in them during most of each year makes them appreciate even more the Hill Country's flowing water—the extrav-agant springs that gush forth here and there along the Escarpment that forms the region's eastern edge, dividing it neatly from the prairies, and farther upland the clear rippling streams that thread their way along the main valleys over white bedrock and gravel and sand, loud down rapids, thoughtful in deep, cold "blue holes" whose banks are lined with willows and sycamores and knee-rooted cypresses. The Hill Country's limestone water flows somewhat less copiously now than it used to long ago, but it still constitutes a sort of miracle in Texas, where muddy or salty or pol-luted or dried-up waterways are what most people know from day to day. And for city Texans, a category that includes the majority of us now, the hills and trees and grass and wildflowers and air and neat aged German farmsteads of limestone and log are all as miraculous as the streams.

Nor is the feeling that Texans have for the Hill Country anything new. It goes back, old memoirs and reminiscences tell us, far into the open-country time before barbed wire, when farming and small-town families in summer—business slack, corn and cotton laid by and needing no more work till harvest—would travel perhaps for days in covered wagons to camp a while beside the Pedernales or the Blanco or the Guadalupe or the Llano or some other of the limpid hill streams. There, unbothered by any-one, they would fish and swim and climb cliffs and pick flowers and ex-plore caves and eat and nap and invite their souls in the cool shade of big pecan trees, all free of charge . . . .

In our own more commercial times, in resort areas along those same rivers—maybe especially on the string of reservoirs that in recent years have stilled the big Colorado's flow through the area—charge to visitors is a more integral part of the pattern, being indeed many genial hill residents' main source of revenue. But except on the lakes and in zones of sub-urbanization near cities lying just below the Escarpment, only a little development is of a flashy or pervasive sort. The Hill Country's charm is quiet, and it tends to induce a taste for quiet pleasures in those who go there.

And outside the developed places, cedar hills doze and animals feed and streams talk and birds sing and seasons change, and those men who intrude, as owners and users for the most part, have mainly come to terms with what this particular kind of land can yield for them at this point in its history and no longer try to strain its usefulness. By its very ruggedness and its resistance to ordinary sorts of human exploitation, at least in modern times, most of the Hill Country has managed to keep change gradual and has preserved much of what makes people like it. The heartland still exists, which is more than you can say these days for a lot of other things from out of the past.

Even gradual change, of course, can add up to big change over a period of time, and the Hill Country has been much altered since white men first came here to stay, a short 130 or so years ago even in the earliest settled parts. That is barely a blink in the real history of the region, whose consideration would involve summoning up a time of molten rocks and steam and lifelessness, and from there threading our way forward through hundreds of hazy millions of years of risings and fallings of the land's surface, and the invasion and recession of numberless fecund seas depositing sediment and organic trash to turn to stratified stone which then was hacked rough by rain and wind and roots and waterflow. And creatures, from the first oozers and squirters and crawlers and swimmers and slitherers on down through great stupid reptiles in swamps and later, big mammals—elephants and ground sloths and giant bison and the like—and the earliest men, who possibly got here from the Bering Strait in time to hunt such beasts with frail stone-tipped weapons before the beasts themselves died out and were supplanted by lesser species . . . All that, and then millennia of probably intermittent occupancy by the varying ancestors of the people we generally call Indians because historic errors linger in language, and finally, in the centuries leading to our own brief era, the Indians themselves divided into tribes and language groups as Europeans found them. We are, we historic Texans of old-world origin, only a minor *John* blink. *Graves*

Yet such is human nature that the blink of what we are concerns us more than all the rest. . . . For a good long period before Europeans began to occupy the continent, the Hill Country together with large parts of ad-joining regions appears to have lain under the sway of an Indian people—wandering hunters and gatherers rather than farmers—who show up in historic times as the tribal group known as Tonkawa. As everyone knows, all American Indians in the end were losers, but the Tonkawas evidently started being losers early, and did the most drastic part of their losing not to white men but to other Indians. Chiefly these were nomadic Co-manches, whose acquisition of horses in the seventeenth century gave them explosive impetus and turned the southern Great Plains into their empire, where they made life miserable for other sorts of people, includ-ing Tonkawas. In addition, the once-prosperous "Tonks" were pressed on also by still other tribes, among them some like the Lipan Apaches who themselves had been chased out of ancestral Plains haunts by the dynam-ic and intolerant Comanche imperialists.

It made for quite a stew in the hills and roundabout, though little of it was witnessed and recorded by whites. In the face of the Comanche threat, Spaniards and Mexicans were mainly content not to wander much north and west of San Antonio, and by the 1840's, when, despite Comanches, land-hungry Anglo-Americans and Germans began moving in numbers up along the Balcones Escarpment and into the hills, the Tonks had been decimated. During the ensuing years of struggle between white and red imperialists, both Tonks and Lipans through their own hatred of Co-manches often served as allies and guides and scouts to the white frontiers-men—not that they received much reward for it. Soon they became scroungy hangers-on around the white settlements, mendicant and thiev-ing and demoralized, looked down on not only for being Indians but for such specific habits as the Tonks' occasional practice of ritual ingestion of fallen enemies. Finally the few who were left were put on a reservation on the upper Brazos, then taken to Oklahoma, where during an 1862 uproar more than half the remaining Tonkawas were massacred by a mob of Shawnees and Creeks and Delawares, for obscure reasons. They were not a popular or lucky race.

In the wrinkled Hill Country where before their troubles started Tonks had hunted and played and lounged and watched their women work, the 15

first white interlopers to show up in numbers were German, and they happened to alight here through a sort of large historic bungle. German settlement of excellent farmland between the Brazos and the Colorado a hundred or so miles east of the Hill Country had begun in the 1830's, and reports of its success had waked enormous interest in Texas among farmers and artisans and others in the old country, which was to stimulate immigration during most of the nineteenth century. In the early forties a high-minded if perhaps unworldly group of German noblemen founded an organization called the Society for the Protection of German Immigrants in Texas, whose purpose was to settle large numbers of Teutons on a huge grant of land between the Llano and upper Colorado rivers, where unfortunately none of the sponsors or their representatives had ever set a noble foot. In furtherance of this philanthropy, between 1844 and 1846 the Society—usually known as the Verein, which means the same thing in German—brought well over 7,000 settlers to Texas. But the grant, besides being rocky and drouthy and unsuited for agriculture, was infested with Comanches who considered it their own and who in those days of scarcely challenged imperial power had no inclination or reason to tolerate intruders. For that matter, in keeping with the flavor of the whole venture, the Verein's own title to it turned out to be faulty, and when the scheme collapsed into bankruptcy in 1847, disgruntled prospective beneficiaries of its plan were strewn all the way from old Indianola on Matagorda Bay to the Edwards Plateau proper.

However, during the period when the grant's inhospitality was becoming evident, the Verein had founded a couple of interim settlements for them—New Braunfels, just below the Escarpment between Austin and San Antonio, and Fredericksburg, in the hills to the northwest not far south of the Llano, where the grant's lower boundary would have lain if it had existed. In these places many of the Germans, shut off from Anglo-Texans' freedom of choice and movement by their language and their culture and their ignorance of the new continent, decided to stay and socked in philosophically to build themselves homes and farms.

The hills were virgin then, of course, and full of richness that showed. The valleys had good soil and timber and brimming fish-full streams. The slopes and rounded hilltops had little brush but were padded with thick flower-sprinkled grass that sustained multitudes of edible wild ruminants as well as the predators—bears and wolves and panthers—who enjoyed that edibility. Wild mustang grapes hung down for making wine, and the climate was milder than any the immigrants had known at home. New country has a prodigal magnificence that not many of us now are ever likely to see. But the Germans saw it in the hills and found no objection to staying there.

Together with Castroville—a non-Verein colony of mainly Alsatian Germans west of San Antonio—the settlements at Fredericksburg and New Braunfels were nodes from which Germans spread out through much of the Hill Country during the years and decades that followed. Coping with Indians as best they could (their record in such relations was rather honorable considering the time and the place), they rooted themselves in the region, often evincing their intention to remain by building thick-walled houses and barns of slab limestone. They held onto some old-world things like draft oxen and brewing and winemaking and beekeeping and well-tended gardens and orchards and massive German meals, but willingly shucked off other old habits and crops that did not work in this land, while taking on new ones that did. Farming in the stream valleys where the region's only deep soils lay, they adopted corn and later cotton as main crops and learned soon to use the hills for grazing livestock. They labored hugely, whole families of them together, and a glance today at what they left can show that they labored well. Villages and mills and roads were built, and so firmly did Germans fix themselves in the Hill Country that their descendants still constitute the basic element of the population in the oldest counties there.

In the earliest years of their presence, the hill Germans were not much bothered with competition from Anglo-American settlers, who were pouring into richer sections up the length of the blackland prairies and elsewhere with that liquid flowing force that the frontier had always had, pausing only momentarily to consolidate against Indians or to learn to cope with new kinds of land, leapfrogging one another on into the fertile wilderness. But in the fifties some started leapfrogging into the Hill Country too, chiefly into parts of it at some distance from the Germans' main areas of settlement. Most were slaveless Southern yeomen, and some like the Germans were primarily farmers, looking for valley land to own and work. The majority at first, however, were cattlemen, with some horseraisers, who cared little whether they owned any land at all as long as they could run their herds, varying in size from moderate to huge, on the unfenced vastness of the hills where the animals mingled and were gathered a couple of times a year for sorting and branding and castration.

longhorns' wild recalcitrance by dilution of their blood, old-style cowboying was on the wane and there was much to reminisce about. The Hill Country's white folks, like its Tonks before them, now had some "good old days" to recall.

On the small farms of the region in the years following the war, cotton had entrenched itself as a main market crop, though most Germans clung for a long time to remnants of the self-sufficient diversity that had marked their farming from the start, planting patches of wheat and corn and vegetables and sorghum in addition to cash cotton. Increasingly, though, diverse or not, it was an extractive sort of farming and hard on the land. Not even the Germans, in the heady decades of possessing immensely fertile new soil, had preserved the careful old-country ways of manuring fields and rotating crops and guarding dirt against erosion, while the Anglos had a couple of centuries of disastrous frontier agricultural tradition behind them when they arrived here. Hence gradually the valley field soils lost their fluffy humus texture, and blew, and washed, and yielded less.

On the hills, what happened was as bad or probably worse. The ruinous overstocking of open-range times had destroyed much of the thick ground cover, and on most places even after fencing began, a memory of primal richness made owners keep putting too many animals in their pastures. Over time, inches or feet of what had been turf-protected topsoil, built over thousands of years from plant and animal residues and limestone, in its turn washed and blew away, and bare rock showed through, and cedar and other scrub moved up out of the ravines and off the cliff-faces to take over, and the thick rich grasses had become, as the song says, sweet memory. Cheated of the water the grass and the soil had soaked in and fed out slowly through hillside springs (it ran off now in destructive floods), streams that had never before stopped flowing began to go dry during rainless periods, unless they were lucky enough to be nourished from deeper water-bearing formations with artesian overflow. Richness had not lasted long.

Mercifully, cotton played out in the Hill Country during the early years of this century, doomed not only by soil exhaustion but by boll weevils and market peculiarities, and cattle diminished in favor of swelling flocks of sheep and mohair goats, weed and scrub eaters better suited to what the range had now become. A pattern of hard-bitten, usually small mixed ranching, with forage crops if any sowed in the old fields, started replacing the former moderately prosperous diversity. Though many

German gardens and orchards and farmsteads were still models of old-world neatness, the tone of life in them was changing to something less organic and self-sustaining and satisfying. The land's own fatigue was souring human existence on it; for that matter, the times themselves turned restless as the nation girded itself for twentieth-century booms and wars and change.

Itchy sons and daughters on growing up often moved away to towns and cities, maybe in other regions; parents on growing old had to give over the fight to keep on making tired land produce without help, and sometimes sold out—a thing almost unknown in former years among Germans, when it had been axiomatic that they hardly ever put land on the market. In Anglo sections—not that the old cultural distinctions were so sharp now as they had once been, much rubbing-off and intermarriage having taken place—people were leaving in even greater numbers, or sometimes turning into semi-migratory cedar-post choppers, a new tough breed adapted to a new tough resource. Changes like these have been taking place all over this country in the present century, but they started happening earliest and were most pronounced in hard-used marginal places like these hills.

Some of the sold farms and ranches were gathered into larger tracts, and some— more and more in recent times—came into the hands of city folks from San Antonio or Austin or Houston, who usually wanted them less for what they would produce than for their quietness and quaintness and beauty, to be savored during vacations and after retirement. Full many a solid, stolid, weathered rock farmhouse today, scarred perhaps by old Indian bullets and by the scratchings of generations of children, has bright new paint on its trim and on weekends listens inwardly to hi-fi music and sophisticated talk. Full many another reposes in the hands of a speculative interim owner, awaiting some nostalgic urban buyer with plenty of cash in the bank, for ironically much of this rough, hard-used land sells now for several times what it was worth when most productive. . . .

With less intensive use the Hill Country got some rest at last, and with rest a sort of muted richness crept back in, less prodigal and less usable than the old lost virgin richness, fostering a diversity of wildlife and plants adapted to the new and more secret world of cedar and scrub and little lost valleys with streams. Hundreds of species of birds found this scheme of things to their liking, and what some old Anglos used to call "short varmints"—coons and foxes and ringtails and such— teemed along the creeks and cliffs. Long varmints that ate big meat having vanished with the frontier itself, brush-loving deer multiplied to numbers unknown in virgin times. Even the springs and watercourses, it seems, revived a bit and grew stronger than they had been in worst era of soil exhaustion and bared hills. Pretty, flowering bushes and weeds spread widely—"useless" plants for the most part, but that was the main reason they were still here to spread and flower. The heartland had become what it is today.

It would be more or less impossible to pick out a typical spot in the Texas Hill Country, for like any interesting region it is quite varied. Some sections are chiefly Anglo in population, in others the old German stock may heavily predominate, and here and there Latin elements are well established. In parts like the area near Fredericksburg and along some of the rivers, stream valleys tend to be wider and there are relatively generous expanses of arable land, often turfed now with tame meadow grasses. But in perhaps most places the hills shoulder against one another, and in the restricted valleys between them flat patches of soil that used to be— occasionally still are—plowed and sowed and harvested, are small in size and scattered. The hills themselves in many areas are still coated with the cedar and Spanish oak and other brush that took over in the era of exhaustion; elsewhere since World War II ranchers have hired bulldozers to scour away these picturesque thickets and have sowed native and exotic range grasses to establish a diminished semblance of what the hills once were. Annual rainfall on the eastward-facing part of the Escarpment is a good five inches more than in the region's western reaches that merge with the main Edwards Plateau, a difference reflected in many ways by vegetation and wildlife. Despite all such variations, though, it may be worth our while to take a look at one small piece of the Hill Country and to ponder its history and character and ways, whether they be typical or not.

It is a little over 250 acres of hillside and valley land lying on Barton Creek in Travis County, not far from the Escarpment and only about twelve miles due west of the state capitol building in Austin, though the nature of the country between them makes the traveling distance quite a bit longer than that, and in terms of the difference in atmosphere it might as well be a hundred miles. Most people now who know the tract call it "Paisano," as did the late Texas writer J. Frank Dobie, its last individual owner and user, who had it and loved it for a few years before his death in 1964 and gave it the Mexican name of his personal totem bird, the gray and swift and gallant chaparral cock, or roadrunner. But during most of its history as a boundaried property it has been know locally as "the Wende place," after the family who owned it longest and got their living from what it produced.

In terms of potential usefulness, it is a rather good piece of land as such small places go in that neighborhood, though in honesty that is not saying much. The neighborhood is a very rocky and hilly one, and if Paisano has relatively little of the sorriest hill soil, the thin eroded stuff inches deep over rock that soil scientists call "Brackett," it also has only about twenty acres of flat deep land fit for cultivation, in three small parcels nestled along the creek and its tributary branches—which is not a large proportion of 250 acres. . . . Except in the vicinity of some superb stone cliffs beside these streams, dark with cedar and other trees and bushes and capped with thick Edwards limestone, the hillsides on the place are not extremely steep, which means that they may have lost somewhat less soil than more sloping land in the old years of overuse.

And in fact, on these gentler uplands of the place, cleared of cedar in the 1950's before Mr. Dobie owned it and little grazed since then, there is good grass cover again, even though it is made up of shorter species—little bluestem and the gramas and mesquitegrass and the like—than the big blue and Indiangrass and switchgrass that ruled in the beginning on such pieces of range in this eastern, wetter section of the Hill Country, often eye-high to a Comanche pony, with lesser grasses and wildflowers thick in their understory. This lush, diverse mat covered all but the steepest, rockiest hills and protected the soil it had built over ages, dotted with live oaks here and there, a savanna. But an excess of cattle ate it down and destroyed it, and the soil lay exposed to erosion, and what ages had built a few decades sufficed to undo. The original tall grasses show up on Paisano now only in occasional clumps and patches, and on the hillsides lie rough pieces of chunk rock, once partly or wholly buried beneath rich earth whose organisms slowly ate on them, and in some places white ledges that the Tonks never glimpsed peer through in further evidence of history's attrition.

Of the people who served as tools of that history, living on the place and working it in the days when it was worked, some knowledge has come down, though full of gaps and often more tantalizing than informative, in the manner of most data on half-seen long-dead people and the events that marked their lives. They were quiet people, not world-shakers. Their lives here were working lives, spent outside the mainstream of forces that swayed their time, or maybe, most lives being thus, they were part of a mainstream that did rule their time and their world, without ever knowing it. . . .

The basic part of the place (additional rough acreage was tacked onto it at some later date) is a rectangle of land that was claimed by one James S. Burton in 1860 under a new state land law. In a survey made for him the following year it is described as containing 160 acres, a quarter-section, but as laid out on the ground the rectangle actually covers a little over 200 acres. Burton has been described somewhere as a speculator, and it is possible that he may have managed to introduce a little hanky-panky into the surveyor's work, but quite possible also that he didn't have to. The old original surveys of wild land were rough and tended to be generous, and a bonus of forty acres or so would not have been much out of line.

At any rate Burton got it, and a jewel of a spot it must have been, for people had been slow to move up into the hills from the fertile black prairies around Austin, the German "nodes" were distant, and main settlement in this section did not get moving in earnest till the Civil War and after. Thus the valley was intact—its little network of streams full of clear water and fish, its bears and deer and panthers and mustangs and turkeys and other creatures well fed and numerous, its grasses thick and tall on spongy soil, its timber virgin, everything still whole. Did his speculative soul allow him to take note of all this? Did he, that spring he made application for its ownership, visit the place with eyes that saw and ears that heard, and did he observe bluebonnets and white-flowered wild plum and honeybees working the horsemint blossoms and listen to redbirds and warblers and from Barton's ledged cliffs the wild falling song of the canyon wren? . . . Whether he did or not, he must have been neither a romantic esthete nor a farmer, for he never lived on the place, and sold it in 1863 to a man with the Germanic name of Frederick Kunze.

About Kunze no significant wisps of information have come down, though it can be surmised that he was *not* strictly speculative in his aims, since he built a stout small house of hewn elm logs on the property, standing on a pleasant rise within a bend of Barton Creek among live oaks and cedar elms and facing southeast with its back to winter northers. Nor is it possible to keep from wondering futilely why, having established himself, he would have sold out to another German, John Daniel Wende, in 1865. . . . Comanches, conceivably—they were active nearby in the 1860's, though no specific record of depredations in this neighborhood during that period seems to exist. (Tales do survive here of Indians who would come to the settlers' cabins and hang around and beg for milk and sweets and things and sometimes pilfer movable objects, but these would have been Tonkawas or Lipans or members of some of the other ruined tribal fragments drifting about on the frontier before disappearing for good.) Or political discord, or the bandit renegades known to have raided up along the Colorado out of Austin during the Civil War. Or bad health, or a discontented wife. . . Frederick Kunze's spouse Lucy could not write, and signed the deed to Wende with a forthright X.

John Daniel Wende's life, on the other hand, outlines itself a bit more clearly for our eyes, because he lived here a long while and had descendants and in-laws and neighbors to remember him. Though unspectacular in any known respect, he was not an average sort of immigrant. He seems to have come from Posen, now Poznan, a part of western Poland that in the mid-nineteenth century was in the hands of Prussia, and he had done quite a bit of traveling around before he settled on Barton Creek. As a young man he learned the miller's trade, and in 1849—a time of uprisings and harsh suppressions in Germany, though whether that fact influenced him I do not know—he went to gold-rush California. There he appears to have forsaken milling temporarily, since it is noted that when he returned to Posen in 1858 he had for some years operated a vinegar factory. Staying at home for only a year or less, he came to Texas near Austin in 1859, ranching and raising horses for a while and later helping to run a gristmill in the Cedar Valley settlement quite close to upper Barton Creek, which makes it almost certain he got to know the neighborhood and probably this place itself at that time.

When war came, like many of the Escarpment Germans he joined the Confederate Army, and was sent to Brownsville on the Rio Grande as a saddlemaker—his talents, it is evident, being quite various. There he struck up friendship with another young German Confederate named Wuthrich, who while on furlough in Austin met and married a Wisconsin German girl born in West Prussia (who on her part had been visiting relatives in Austin and was stranded there by the war's turmoil). After a three-day honeymoon, the unlucky Wuthrich went back alone to duty at Brownsville, where he died of some sickness without ever seeing his bride **25** again. Carrying the sad news to Austin, John Wende liked Mary Schemmel Wuthrich and was liked in return, and in July of 1865, having been released from the defeated army and like most discharged soldiers ready to begin a settled life, married her. Two months later they bought the Barton Creek place from enigmatic Frederick and Lucy Kunze and went to live on it. It is a brief tale to tell but a nice one, and you could build a novel on it, with people wandering around far from different homes and building solid lives on accident. But it was not more remarkable than many such patterns in nineteenth-century America.

If this part of the hills was new and fresh in those days, it was nevertheless not lonesome, for settlement was well under way. Travis County and Hays, which begins only a short distance south of the Wende place, were never "German counties" in the sense of having particularly large numbers of these immigrants in their populations. However, this section held a good sprinkling of them. John George Rissmann, an Alsatian, was one of the earliest settlers at Cedar Valley, having come there by 1855 from the Castroville colony, and a glance at a map of original surveys in the Paisano neighborhood is revealing. Alongside old British surnames like Moore and Morgan and Bradford and Frazier and Harris and Young and Fawcett, you find in just about equal numbers such families as Trautwein, Heinson, Dittmar, Bohls, Hartwig, and Ottens. Nor is there much discernible clustering of Germans with Germans and Anglos with Anglos; the names are stirred together into a rich cartographic hodge-podge.

Cultural differences were strong then, with even the languages separate. By preference the Wendes must certainly have sought the company of Teutons like the Rissmanns (their daughter later married one) and the Hartwigs, who were near neighbors. (So near, in fact, that in the absence of fences they mislocated the property line and erected their cedar-log house partly on their own place and partly on the Wendes'; it stands there abandoned today, skewered by the east boundary fence, which was stretched after a modern survey. . . .) But in such a neighborhood the two breeds undoubtedly came to know each other better and exchanged ways of doing things more quickly than they did in sections where apartness was sharper. In most of the Hill Country, for instance, it is generally said that in the days before wire nearly all stone fences were built by and for Germans, entire families laboring sometimes for years on end to get field land or even whole farms enclosed, or if they were rich enough hiring crews of professional German wall-builders to do it for them at three or

four hundred dollars a mile. Anglo-Texans traditionally preferred split-
rail fences, cheaper and faster to build even if quicker to deteriorate. Yet
in the Wende neighborhood you can visit the place of an Anglo family who
have been there since things began, and as you talk with a weathered
bright old man about the way things used to be in his father's day and his
grandfather's, most fences within reach of your gaze, besides some newer
stretches of goat wire, are of age-blackened limestone slabs laid by his
forebears' hands.

Be all that as it may, a man who had gotten around as much in the New
World as John Wende had since first leaving home must have fitted in
easily with the Anglo frontier pattern of mixed open-range stockraising
and small farming. And the farming was definitely small, because even if
for a time he used some of the shallow-soiled pasture slopes as cropland,
a frequent practice, they are bound to have washed rather soon, after
which he was back down to what farmland he had really had from the beginning, twenty good acres in three small fields nestled beside the creeks,
sowed annually to three or four standard crops plus a garden. ("They
raised corn and cotton and sorghum cane, like all the rest of us," says the
old Anglo neighbor wryly, calling up hazy childhood when he knew them
as tired old folks, "and plenty of grassburrs and johnsongrass.")

Yet John and Mary Wende clearly had the old-country feeling that they
and their descendants were in this place to stay. They put up good stone
fences, still standing for the most part, around their fertile small fields—
some, ingeniously, on the cliffs above, where the most stones were to be
had. They began adding onto the Kunzes' little elm-log house with stone
and later with planks, a process that has gone on into the reigns of modern
owners and has left the old log part invisible within the pleasant higglety-
pigglety galleried structure that stands there today. And they moved
ahead with all the other work, besides tending fields and stock, that bringing new land into shape entails—clearing out timber, establishing roads
into the place and between its parts, digging out and boxing a spring (a
nice one still flows most of the time on the branch beside the house), con-
structing outbuildings and pens, and the rest. Maybe Wende exercised in
the area one of his various skills as miller, as vinegar-maker, as saddler or
whatever, to make extra money and hire help in some of this work, for the
Wende children, a daughter and son born in 1867 and 1872, can't have
been big enough to be of much use during the hardest period. Local lore
does hold faint memory of a man, probably hired, who lived with the **27**

Wendes for a time, and died, and was buried on the place in a spot nobody now alive remembers. But concerning the main pattern of work and who laid what stretch of stone wall where and all that, no real information has lingered down, nor does it matter much. What is certain is that the work got done, for many of its results still show today.

In 1877, twelve years after they had bought the place, the Wendes engaged in a somewhat curious transaction which lodged itself in legal reccords—John Wende assigned all his worldly goods to his wife Mary's ownership, possibly because of debt or a pending lawsuit or something on that order. Besides the Barton Creek land and some implements and effects, the list mentions sixteen horses, sixty head of cattle, and fifteen hogs, which are at least seven or eight times as many animals as the place would carry today and a good many more than it ought to have been made to carry then. Wende was using the open range, of course, of which most of his own place was a part, and if others roundabout were using it as hard or harder, as almost certainly they were, the country was already overloaded. And the dwindling of the open range, due to begin with wire in the eighties, would in homesteaded areas like this make things even worse, for men accustomed to running that many beasts kept trying to run nearly as many within their own newly fenced small tracts, disastrously.

Another item of property conveyed to Mary Wende at this time was thirty acres of land in, of all places, Johnson County, Kansas. Clearly at one time or another John Daniel Wende had done more moving around than shows up in our record. . . .

He lived out his life on this little hill place, using up its richness while it used up his manhood, and died in 1897 after having dwelt and labored here for thirty-two years. The region's time of exhaustion was beginning —or was beginning to show, for in truth it had begun when settlement did. After his father's death the son, John Charles, then twenty-six, waited only till the next year before giving up the fight and leaving this place where Wendes had come to stay and had laid up stones on stones to prove it. His mother stayed for a time in the neighborhood with her daughter Mrs. Rissmann, and neighbors remember the two of them coming over to the place for a day's outing in the manner of ladies reliving family memories. Then she moved to Austin, where she later died.

The property was farmed and grazed occasionally after that—by tenants, by neighbors who leased it, and once even by John Charles Wende, who returned for a year or so. But nobody used it hard any more, for its ability to reward hard use was gone. It was furring over with cedar and scrub, its tall grasses gone, its hillsides stony, its creeks shrunken or dry in bad summers, its field soils' fertility numbed. Only a little while after civilized men had come here to stay, it lay depleted and tired out and not really worth utilizing any longer in cash American terms, as did much of the whole region of which it was a part.

I suppose it would be easy enough to wax prim about this, in our hindsighted aftertime. But the pattern that predestined the Hill Country's exhaustion was an ancient one, not just American but human. Virgin land has intoxicated herders and farmers since whenever such activities began, and has seduced them into believing its lushness would last forever, and they have used it hard. Even in easily despoiled parts of the world like these hills, the land's decline under such treatment, though rapid in geological or merely historical terms, has usually been gradual enough that men could lull themselves into not seeing it until too late. And if indeed they saw it, they were themselves often stuck in the pattern too—through habit, through the disappearance of frontiers. Hence the bared hills of Texas and Lebanon and Greece, and the starkness of much of once-fertile Spain and of those Balkans that were the Romans' granary, and the lateritic desolation of cleared tropical rainforest lands, and the sad decline of practically all vulnerable parts of the whole poor bloody old earth, whose virginity no longer exists simply because one of its millions of biological experiments developed a conquering brain, and hands.

The Wende place's fertility at any rate, like that of many another piece of land, had served to launch a family on its way in the New World. It was sold in the 1920's to the first of three or four latter-day owners, mainly absentee, who seem to have sought not so much profit as pleasure from it, though the last of them before Frank Dobie bought it did put effort into restoring some of its usefulness, having the smoother parts cleared of cedar and sowing them to new grass. This fact in turn may have predisposed Mr. Dobie to appreciation of its beauty, for not only did he admire grass like any old cattleman, but cedar's winter pollen gave him intense hay fever. Though living still in Austin, in his last years he focused his lifelong fascination with honest earth on this small piece of it, and made ritual alterations of the house as all other owners had done, and wrote and reflected here and listened to creatures and water, and had friends out for whiskey and steaks and good talk, congenial gatherings which those of us who attended them recall now with nostalgic pleasure.

He also continued the work of restoration on the place, conferring with government range specialists and often exulting over a reestablished patch of big bluestem or switchgrass. But his view of such things was not economic, and he could get just as much pleasure out of a clump of blooming prickly pear or an agarita bush or a gray fox or any of a thousand other live things belonging in this (despite history) lush corner of the hills. As far as I ever knew, his only real stab at "using" Paisano in any standard fashion was an experiment with sheep undertaken in partnership with a sheep-wise friend. As a cowman by birth, he had some suspicion of these small fleecy beasts, but he observed them carefully and did some pleasant writing about their habits, though I believe he ended with much the same feeling he had when he started. "When an animal without brains also lacks instinct," he wrote concerning a ewe that would not suckle her lamb, "the nadir of all negatives is reached."

After Mr. Dobie died in 1964 Paisano was bought up by subscription and turned over to the care of the University of Texas, a circumstance which together with some neighboring old-timers' reluctance to sell out has thus far saved the valley from the sort of exurban ranchette development that is increasing on hills not far away. (The new city hill-folks like high sites with wide views, whereas the old ones took their views while chasing cows and built their houses low, near water and good soil. . . .) A Dobie memorial, the place serves now as a residence-retreat for creative people on fellowships—painters and writers and photographers and the like— who come there individually with their families if they have families, to work and live for a year, taking on proprietorship as their awareness of the place's peacefulness and functioning and secrets and muted, latter-day magnificence grows.

They hear owls, and mating squalling ringtails, and unobstructed country thunder, and swift Barton among its stream-bed stones and ledges and potholes, and the multitudinous birds of the Texas hill spring, and the snort and thump of deer surprised on hillsides, and many other natural sounds that men have been hearing in this valley since men have been coming here, even if at this late date a few of the old sounds that tickled the ears of speculative James S. Burton and enigmatic Frederick Kunze are missing and likely will remain so. They see and ponder wild plums and prairie flowers, and cedars rooting themselves in cracks or pockets of soil on cliffs where feral Spanish goats dwell, and the little fields once plowed with teams of horses (parklike now, with heavy grass) and protected by

John Daniel Wende's grayed rock fences, and the ways of flowing water *John*
in floodtime and drouth and through the seasons, and Indian flints, and *Graves*
fossils, and the rotting but still erect shapeliness of the log Hartwig house
that stands astraddle the east boundary fence in commemoration of its
builders' old mistake. . . . And if they care anything at all for what they
hear and see and ponder here, as most have, they come to their own sort
of comprehension of the valley and the hills and their history and their
wholeness, and comprehending they own.

It is not a bad sort of ownership for the place to have these days, after
all it has known before. Men dwell softly on this land again, and it was
time for that.

THE PHOTOGRAPHER'S INTRODUCTION

Jim Bones, Jr. **P**hotographs, like everything else we see, are fugitive illusions derived from light. It causes mist to rise, wind to blow, and rain to water the land. Scattering, sunlight makes the sky blue, and striking chlorophyll, it makes green plants grow. Animals harvest its energy as blades and stems and seeds. Gas, oil, coal, plastics, minerals, and metals, all are vibrating atoms of light. The atmosphere, the oceans, the very rocks of the planet are the distillate dross of our star.

Culminating more than ten years of Hill Country study, most of these photographs were taken while I was on an in-residence fellowship at Paisano, a 254-acre nature sanctuary along Barton Creek that was J. Frank Dobie's last country place. The Dobie-Paisano Fellowship is currently offered annually by the Texas Institute of Letters and the University of Texas at Austin to an artist or writer associated with the Southwest.

My Paisano project was to photograph throughout one year the daily details of nature that reveal the changing seasons. This may sound like a lot to ask of scrubby eroded hills, but careful observers may see more of the region's character in these few acres than casual travelers can speeding across the entire Edwards Plateau.

Although little of America's earth is untouched by man, Paisano remains an island of relative wildness in civilization's widening sea. As requested by Bertha McKee Dobie, from the fellowship's inception Paisano has been a nature reserve where no hunting or collecting is allowed. Used lightly and grazed mostly by wildlife, it has regained a significant measure of its natural heritage. Its solitude now offers artists and writers unparalleled opportunity for inspiration.

In August of 1972 I arrived at Paisano with my wife Ann, our dog Omer, and Cloud the white rabbit. Day by day the wild flow enfolded us as we discovered the springs, the branches, the secret places, and what bloomed late for summer or early in the onrushing fall.

On the best days I got up before dawn and went out to greet the rising sun. The softness of morning light, repeated at evening, transfigures the

commonplace with beauty, and often then the wind is still. Though an old
friend to flowering grasses and trees, wind can be my antagonist during
the long exposures that small apertures require. But with good light, mild
breezes, and only a stopwatch for time, I passed whole days searching the
streams, the woods, and the fields for moments to photograph.

I learned about photography from Russell W. Lee and Eliot F. Porter,
who taught how to look for the key patterns of a place in weather, water,
land, vegetation, animals, and changing light. I use a view camera with a
squeeze-bulb shutter release, that sits on a tripod and makes 4 x 5 inch
transparencies. With film holders, filters, and extra lenses, the outfit
weighs about twenty-five pounds, and though it makes superb nature
renderings, it is a warping chore to carry, especially in summer heat.

By mid-September there had been no rain for several weeks and the
hills were tinderbox dry. Near sundown Friday, the anniversary weekend
of Mr. Dobie's death, I watched clouds build slowly to the north. Thunder
rumbled closer, the sky turned brooding dark, and silent tension charged
the air. I was compelled toward the east pasture fence and Omer howled
inside the house. I looked across the field to a live oak a hundred yards
away as a blue-white arc split a fencepost under its twisted limbs. Brilliant
crackling fire balls discharged at nodes along the rusty wires and the wind
whipped a dozen flaming rings outward through the grasses.

I thought of calling for help, but there was no time, so I got an old
blanket and ran to the fence. I beat out one fire, but the others doubled in
size, and apocalyptic visions of the house, the trees, the fields, all raged in
flames before me. Small and alone I realized I was powerless against
nature and prayed for deliverance of the land with its helpless creatures.
Healing rain fell harder and harder, quenching the flames to smoke and
finally to dead black ashes.

Many times that year and since, lightning in different forms has called
my attention to the intricate interwoven powers of the universe. Occasionally awareness has come like the swift wingbeats of rising quail, but
more often like the cascading echoes of canyon wrens.

In October, from cliffs over Barton Creek, I looked down on a cedar elm,
mossy-backed and tall among its kind. The low sun shone through every
yellow leaf, revealing a lace of veins. As I sat breathing deeply, a fiber of
light seemed to grow from the base of the tree where the seed germinated
years ago, unfolding above and below. Briefly each leaf and stem and
branch glowed in a golden tapestry. Fine threads of life from the original **33**

small nightmare hours of early morning the storm finally ended, the temperature climbed slightly, and thawing began. First came sounds of drops, then fragments, and as melting quickened, limbcasts and long stalactites of ice shattered in the breaking day. Branches lifted, trees straightened, grasses swung back to the sky or fell to the stones as binding crystal tubes broke away, and from tree and bush alike, ice leaves dropped to the ground.

Even in apparent chaos an inscrutable order persists, and though many creatures perished in the storm, many more survived. The limbs torn off were rotten at heart, and searching later for wood I found seasoned logs brought down by other glazing rains.

Although darkness reigns at the mid-winter solstice and the sun appears to seek its lowest point, from then on the days grow stronger toward summer light. At dusk the day after Christmas, poachers roped across the northeast edge of Paisano, scattering a small nomadic clan of Spanish goats. At sunrise the next day, I followed Omer's excited barking to a new-born kid, abandoned on the cliffs.

Conceived as we came to Paisano in early August, for five months she had grown in the warm darkness of her mother's belly to be born under Capricorn. Black with brown stockings, Alise had a white angle on her forehead, and though not a native, she was a wild thing with habits bred by many generations, eluding rustlers, snakes, and dogs along the brushy creek. Ann fed her by bottle, and danced with her in the kitchen, and for a while we were her family.

New leaves of bluebonnet and cucumber weed thrived in the wet infant year, when in January the first big snow came. Snow is such a novelty here that people are free to enjoy its purity without grumbling over cold engines or slick streets. Or so I thought, until one February morning I awoke to thunder coming out of the north.

Torrents poured down, lightning played along the hills, and the temperature plunged to near twenty degrees. Obviously it was no ordinary storm, and since I had no film on hand I was obliged to skid into town, leaning around an icy windshield. Soon the rain turned to stinging sleet mixed with fine wet snow, and then to aggregate snowflakes that swirled in heavy waves. Sharp gusts pushed drifts around roots, over rocks, and into mounds of old grass where migrant pine siskins, juncos, and purple finches huddled with resident sparrows.

The sun moved hidden, the wind howled, and the sky raged like a blue-gray sea. A late wave of arctic air thousands of miles long and many miles deep rolled down to the Gulf of Mexico. As the polar night tumbled toward the tropics of the earth countless creatures turned their backs to numbing cold. Feeding on heat, blue northers live as surely as green or furry things, and though we more resemble lichen scales on ancient stone, we too are kin to the storms.

Six-sided crystals fell through the night, weaving a blanket of ice, and by dawn snow draped the limbs and trunks of trees. Delicate flowers of hasty water elms hung lifeless brown. Henbit and draba, blooming two days before, lay frozen on the ground, but Cloud the white rabbit kicked up invisible heels.

After noon a pale sun drifted through ragged clouds and exposed snow melted in the freezing air. At sundown thawing ceased and the day's brief warmth rushed back into space. Under fleeing stars and a clear moon ice curtains descended below dripping springs, frost needles laced over the ground, and thin shelves edged around creek stones.

The sun came up red through a sub-zero dawn and warmed the granular snow to scattered patches. Fragile jewels melted slowly in shadows, henbit and draba bravely bloomed again, and buckeyes opened shiny leaves.

All alive in March, trees swayed, touching the wind on blowing mornings. Live oaks lost their leaves and wild plums flowered soft and white, calling bees with fragrant pollen. In autumn I had seen that spring cannot leap out of nowhere as it sometimes appears, catching us unawares, though many other years I had anxiously waited, fearing for its return before emerald elm leaves unfurled.

Early in April, after the last frost, I went to a stony overlook to see the earth shade the sun. Instead, as I stepped to the rim I glanced down at a huge coil curving under the rock. I stamped on the ledge and jumped away. The scaly head of a snake appeared over the western horizon, but as I offered no threat it turned back to watch the setting sun. The rattler paid little attention as I made photographs and did not move when I touched it.

But later on a warm April day when I met the diamondback again, it moved swiftly to escape. I blocked its path, and coiling and rattling it expressed fear so loudly the sound seemed to pierce my spine. Backing part way over the ledge it made a stand, ready if I advanced to strike and fall. Snakes lead thankless lives, eating prolific rodents, so I gladly stood aside. Shooting straight for a hole by a cedar root the supple body disappeared inside, and then suddenly a few feet away it pushed up through the warming soil.

The snakes were out, the rains had come, and like wild lovers the waters tumbled over the earth's rocky bed. The swollen streams ran clean and clear when Ann and I took to rafting with the R. H. Crawfords on Barton Creek. Alise followed down a grassy bank and, afraid of being left behind, leaped into the water as we cast off. We were all swept down white rapids where she had trouble keeping her head up. I dove in and heaved her onto the spinning raft. Drifting to the crossing she shivered and shook but paid close attention to the trip, perhaps as the first Spanish goat to navigate Barton Creek.

After Alise went ashore at the low-water bridge we raced ahead into unknown waters, and bounced around a bend off a boulder where a weathered cottonmouth was sunning. Shelves of stone cut from an ancient ocean surrounded us like history books with passages recorded before man was born, and along the shifting bottom fossil rocks clicked and murmured.

I had the primitive pleasures of a woodrat basking on floodwrack glad to be alive after a midnight storm, but I also felt a sailor's poetry in burial at sea, rocking softly on ocean swells, a single cell in the Being indivisible. Enchanted with the song of rainwater rushing back to its source, I reached into the strong current and held a splintered sun dancing on waves of light.

Throughout early spring as the living waters surged and ebbed the great seed-making went on. Each wildflower jewel in its way came to bloom, but Alise, not caring for their names, helped herself to many beautiful plants, and converted them into smart little pills of manure. By May a striking magenta flower comes to the rainbow-lace cactus, whose feathery petals each year open only one day, and if it rains then, all hope of seed-making is lost. Lately a lot of rare and lovely lives have been irretrievably lost to nature-loving collectors, professional and amateur, and dead specimens do not reproduce.

Approaching high solstice, the sun fills flowers with light and new-born creatures with innocence. Early one June morning a tiny spotted fawn, confused and distracted by snorts and whistles from skittish does, came straight to me across a field of goldenwaves. Timid, staring curiously, it sniffed, turning attentive ears, alert for signs of danger or kinship. I wanted to reach out and touch it, but I thought, you do not know people.

This is no way for a wild thing to behave, and some fall you will meet a bad end. Starting forward convinced it, and it bolted away.

Four times that day I found wide-eyed fawns bobbing on shaky legs. One cried out like a goat as it fled, but another lay quiet and still, hidden in the waving grass. Within two weeks I could see them only from a distance, as they ran on strong legs, growing wise in the ways of deer.

A mellow sadness colors ripe summer fields after the green intensity of spring. Almost imperceptibly the sun starts down the days toward long dark winter nights, life busies itself hoarding the light, and acorns fatten to fall.

Well past solstice the heat hangs on and eventually drought sears this semi-arid country, bringing sundowns that flower with dust and whining, droning cicadas. Late summer can be a fitful season of scorched memories and wavering light when creeks dry up, fields wither, and vulture wings beat on stagnant air. Life then is driven within, searching for the strength to survive.

From the dim interior of the living room I watched lonely orphan Alise walk the gallery, little hooves ticking on stone, alone, beautiful, and dear, but grazing in unchecked numbers her kind leave swift desolation. Some say goats have Satan's eyes, maybe for the hellish look they can bring to land, yet the same can be said of sheep and man.

Ecologists say the human pack with its rampant technology threatens to devour life as we know it, and many things pictured in this book have already been lost. The bluebonnets and prickly pear of the frontispiece were buried under an expressway loop, and the whitewater rapids was blasted for a leaky suburban sewer. Because of radioactive plutonium and strontium, the fluorocarbons, chlorinated hydrocarbons, phosphates, mercury, lead, and the like poisoning the earth, it may be too late for us. Human greed and ignorance are the greatest impediments to our making peace with nature, and only a world understanding of the essential interdependence of all things can now prevent disaster.

Most people today do not know what a healthy environment looks like, simply because we never get to see one. So little remains of the wild nature that bore and shaped us that few ever experience peace or natural harmony. However, when we view a place with integrity we know it instinctively by its beauty. In damaged areas we feel the loss of integrity as ugliness, and too often in bitter frustration turn away or add to the damage.

We vitally need the wild places, large and small, where nature demonstrates the basic elements of adaptation, cooperation, and balanced growth. Learning to preserve and appreciate the beautiful patterns of wild places like Paisano can help us to develop an ethical common sense for natural ways. Wildness contains the only extant vestige of the creative order that brought us to life, and wilderness is the last refuge of noble seeds capable of surviving in an everchanging world.

We find ourselves the present caretakers of the earth's wild gardens with freedom to continue down the road to terracide or to alter our course in the direction of harmony. We can take voluntarily a sane path to a smaller population by fewer births, or nature will soon correct the imbalance in catastrophic ways.

Unconsciously we have gotten ourselves crosswise to the cosmos and the going is likely to get worse before it ever improves. But the collective will of humanity evolves from wildness, culture, enlightenment, spirit corporeal, idea made real. Reflecting upon itself to see more clearly, it is a force unique. It remade the face of this planet, reached out to the moon, and now holds the solar fires in its hands. What fate will it choose? Which side will it cherish, the darkness or the light of the infinite One that is both?

Paradoxically, in wild pursuit of life we leave the greatest mark in what we leave untouched. So save for the children's sake a little unspoiled land, and love and grace and green leaves may in time heal the wounded earth.

PLATES

J. Frank Dobie **H**ere I am living on a soil that my people have been living and working and dying on for more than a hundred years—the soil as it happens of Texas. My roots go down into this soil as deep as mesquite roots go. This soil has nourished me as the banks of the lovely Guadalupe River nourish cypress trees, as the Brazos bottoms nourish the wild peach, as the gentle slopes of east Texas nourish the sweet-smelling pines, as the barren, rocky ridges along the Pecos nourish the daggered lechuguilla. I am at home here, and I want not only to know about my home land, I want to live intelligently on it. I want certain data that will enable me to accommodate myself to it. Knowledge helps sympathy to achieve harmony.

Viguiera goldeneyes, sunflowers, and a cedar elm in early autumn fog

Plate 1

Dawn mist rising over Barton Creek

Plate 2

Leaves, vapors, shadows, and reflections

Plate 3

Cottonmouth water moccasin

Plate 4

Sunflowers, goldeneyes, ice-weeds, switchgrass, and tumbled boulders Plate 5

Maximilian sunflowers, cardinal flowers, and maidenhair fern Plate 6

Mustang grape, plane-tree sycamore, and wild dogwood leaves

Plate 7

Sundown thunderstorms

Plate 8

Twin lightning bolts

Plate 9

Standing waves at a narrow place

Plate 10

Muddy flood around sycamores

Plate 11

Abandoned creek channels and clearing storm   Plate 12

Palafoxia, ragweed, spiked grama grass, and stones   Plate 13

Argiope orb-weaver spider and dew

Plate 14

Autumn sunrise

Plate 15

Frost on drift in Little Grape Creek

Plate 16

Hoarfrost on ticklegrass and Spanish oak leaves

Plate 17

Jackfrost on twisted leaf yucca

Plate 18

Frost on old sycamore leaves and embryo buds   Plate 19

Creek grasses and reflections   Plate 20

Willows, plane trees, cedar elms, and switchgrass

Plate 21

Cedar-elm branches, creek bank, and cliffs

Plate 22

Cedar-elm leaves on mossy stone

Plate 23

Spanish oak, cedar, and bluestem grass   Plate 24

Reflected autumn sundown   Plate 25

Sedge, Spanish oak, and sycamore leaves in shallow water

Plate 26

Burr oak, cedar, sycamore, cypress, and wild cherry on Colorado River cliffs

Plate 27

Sycamore seeds, cypress leaves, and cypress seeds in the Frio River

Foggy rain on bluestem, feather bluestem, lovegrass, and muhly

Plate 29

December icestorm

Plate 30

Crystal lace on cactus and grass

Plate 31

Leaves of Spanish oak and ice

Plate 32

Paisano house and gate

Plate 33

Frozen ice-weed juices

Plate 34

Hackberry tree and mustang grape vines

Plate 35

Buckeye seedpods

Plate 36

Cedar elm, yaupon, Spanish oak, and sycamore

Plate 37

Light powdered first snow

Plate 38

Snow-covered banks of Barton Creek

Plate 39

Ice curtains below dripping springs

Plate 40

Twisted leaf yucca and buried grasses

Plate 41

Snow on shallow pools

Plate 42

Dwarf palmetto

Plate 43

Snow-lined Spanish oaks

Plate 44

Bluestem grass at sunrise   Plate 45

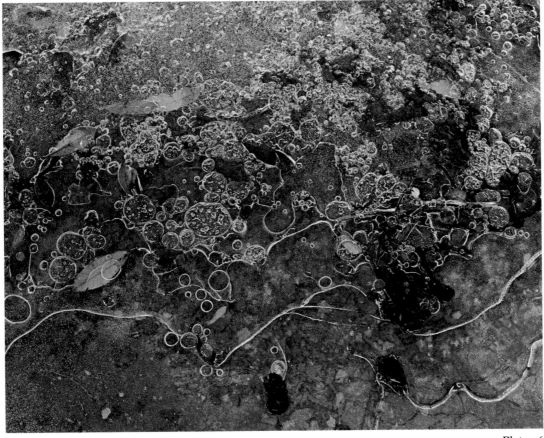

Frozen bubbles   Plate 46

Draba flowers, wet algae, cactus, and grass

Plate 47

Whitewater rapids

Plate 48

Wild plum flowering   Plate 49

Ice-broken redbud blooming   Plate 50

Anemones

Plate 51

Morel mushrooms and acorns

Plate 52

Hackberry branches and Spanish oak catkins   Plate 53

Cretaceous clam and recent leaves   Plate 54

March icestorm   Plate 55

Frosted agarita leaves   Plate 56

Spanish oak leaves

Plate 57

Widow's tears

Plate 58

Cedar sage

Plate 59

Bluebonnets

Plate 60

Buckeyes

Plate 61

Cypress leaves

Plate 62

Plane-tree sycamores   Plate 63

Baby blue-eyes   Plate 64

Beargrass nolina

Plate 65

Diamondback rattler watching sundown

Plate 66

Creek stones and flowing water

Plate 67

April norther

Plate 68

Spring flood at Green Rock

Plate 69

Prickly poppies and Texas thistles

Plate 70

Rainbow lace cactus and yellow sorrel   Plate 71

Spotted fawn in waving grass

Plate 72

Mesquite, coreopsis goldenwaves, lantana, dayflowers, and cone flowers

Plate 73

Wind-twisted cedar on a cliff rim   Plate 74

Summer field   Plate 75

Wild plums

Plate 76

Pothole and scouring stones

Plate 77

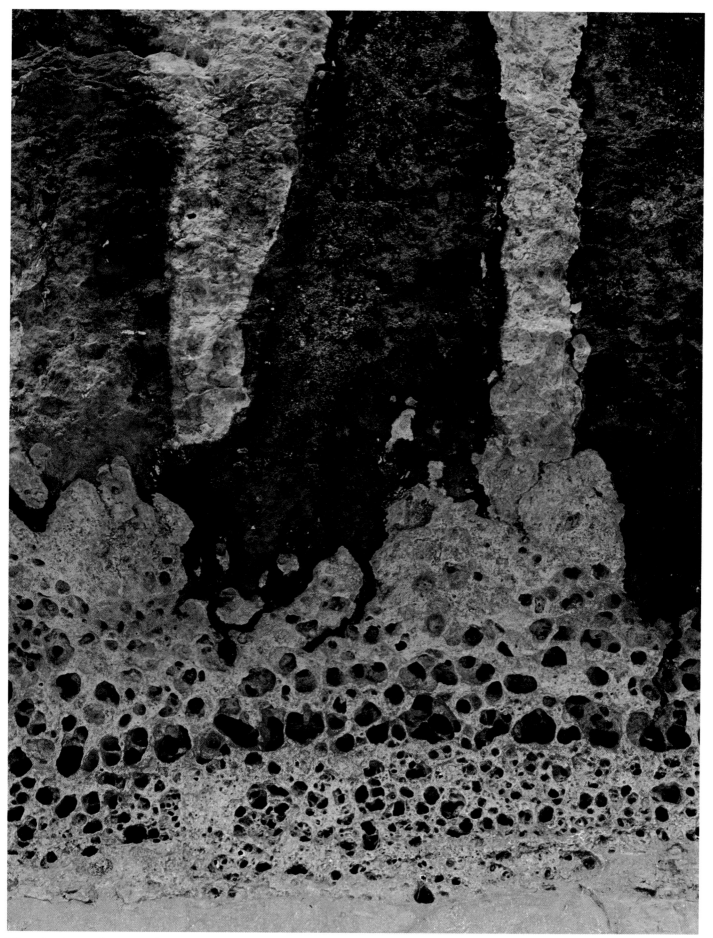

Mineral stains on honeycombed limestone cliffs

Plate 78

Muhly and ticklegrass by Flat Creek

Plate 79

Duststorm   · Plate 80

Prickly pear tunas   Plate 81

Live oak, cedar elm, agarita, prickly pear, bluestem, and early autumn mist

Plate 82